MAZE & SEEK-N-FIND

ABC CITY

Roxie Munro

Schiffer **Kids**™

4880 Lower Valley Road, Atglen, PA 19310

Take a stroll with Chris and his dog Rusty through

Stay on the sidewalk, crosswalks, or a path and find your way from A to Z. Each page flows into the next—it's one continuous route! Along the way, look for the items listed that start with the letters on those pages. The seek-n-find answers are provided in the back of the book. Have fun!

FIND
apple, airplane, ambulance & bicycle, books, balloons, bananas

FIND
cup, cat, clock,
carrots &
dancer,
dinosaurs

FIND
earrings, elephant,
eyeglasses &
flag, flowers,
firetruck

FIND
guitar, gas station, glasses, giraffe & horse, harp, helicopter

GAS

FIND
ice cream, island,
ink pen &
jewelry, jacket,
jaguar

FIND
key, kite, knife &
library, ladder,
laundry

FIND
money, monkeys,
movie theater &
nests, nails,
necktie

FIND
octopus, owl,
oranges &
pig, picnic tables,
penguins

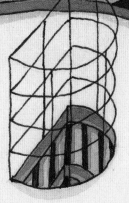

FIND
queen, quadruplets,
question mark &
rabbit, restaurant,
railroad

FIND

school, seesaw,
swing set &
taxi, tennis,
tiger

FIND
unicorn, unicycle,
umbrellas &
violin, vines,
vegetables

FIND
wheelchair, whale, watches &
x-ray, xylophone, x-crossing

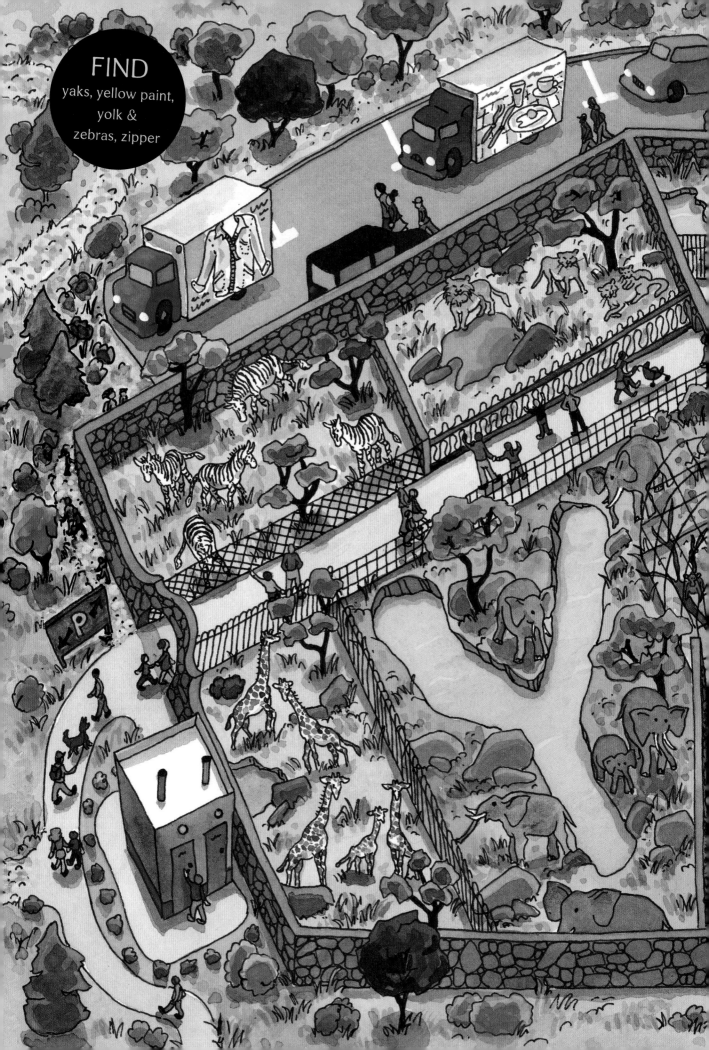

FIND
yaks, yellow paint, yolk & zebras, zipper

ANSWER KEY

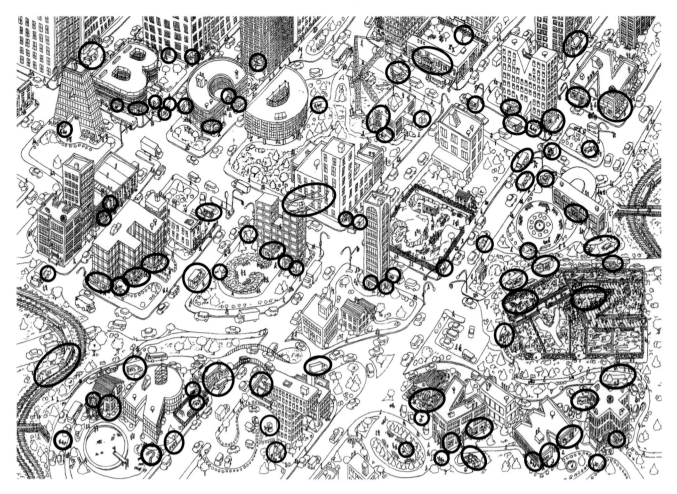

**To my late parents, Robert and Margaret Munro,
who taught me my ABC's early on.**

Thanks to the Bank Street Writers Lab members for a first look at this project.

ISBN: 978-0-7643-6481-5
Printed in India

Published by Schiffer Kids
An imprint of Schiffer Publishing, Ltd.
4880 Lower Valley Road
Atglen, PA 19310
Phone: (610) 593-1777; Fax: (610) 593-2002
Email: Info@schifferbooks.com
Web: www.schifferbooks.com

For our complete selection of fine books on this and related subjects, please visit our website at www.schifferbooks.com. You may also write for a free catalog.

Schiffer Publishing's titles are available at special discounts for bulk purchases for sales promotions or premiums. Special editions, including personalized covers, corporate imprints, and excerpts, can be created in large quantities for special needs. For more information, contact the publisher.

FSC — MIX
Paper from responsible sources
FSC® C016779
www.fsc.org